CHIMPANZEE

WRITTEN BY
E.C. ANDREWS

ENDANGERED
LIFE CYCLES

American adaptation copyright © 2026 by North Star Editions, Mendota Heights, MN 55120. All rights reserved. No part of this book may be reproduced or utilized in any form or by any means without written permission from the publisher.

Chimpanzee © 2024 BookLife Publishing
This edition is published by arrangement with BookLife Publishing

Library of Congress Control Number:
The Library of Congress Control Number is available on the Library of Congress website.

ISBN
979-8-89359-310-5 (library bound)
979-8-89359-394-5 (paperback)
979-8-89359-369-3 (epub)
979-8-89359-340-2 (hosted ebook)

Printed in the United States of America
Mankato, MN
092025

sales@northstareditions.com
888-417-0195

Written by:
E.C. Andrews

Edited by:
Rebecca Phillips-Bartlett

Designed by:
Ker Ker Lee

All facts, statistics, web addresses and URLs in this book were verified as valid and accurate at time of writing. No responsibility for any changes to external websites or references can be accepted by either the author or publisher.

Photo Credits – Images are courtesy of Shutterstock.com. With thanks to Getty Images, Thinkstock Photo and iStockphoto.

Cover – sabine_lj, Arnain, Eric Isselee, VVadi4ka, MIKHAIL GRACHIKOV. Recurring – bum katya, imaginasty, VVadi4ka, sabine_lj, Arnain, VVadi4ka. 4–5 – PCH.Vector. 6–7 – KensCanning, Lilly P. Green. 8–9 – Edwin Butter, PARALAXIS. 10–11 – Ariane Ribbeck, Clinton Moffat. 12–13 – Anton_Ivanov, Oleg Senkov. 14–15 – Patrick Rolands, COULANGES. 16–17 – alterfalter, Gerdie Hutomo. 18–19 – Eric Gevaert, Patrick Rolands. 20–21 – Papa Bravo, PARALAXIS. 22–23 – vitrolphoto, chuchiko17.

CONTENTS

PAGE 4   What Is a Life Cycle?
PAGE 6   Chimpanzees
PAGE 8   Endangered Animals
PAGE 10 The Life Cycle Begins
PAGE 12 Being Born
PAGE 14 Newborns
PAGE 16 Growing Up
PAGE 18 Adult Life
PAGE 20 Dangers
PAGE 22 The Life Cycle Continues
PAGE 24 Glossary and Index

WORDS THAT LOOK LIKE THIS CAN BE FOUND IN THE GLOSSARY ON PAGE 24.

What is a Life Cycle?

Animals, people, and plants are living things. They go through different stages during their lives. They change and grow during each stage. This is called a life cycle.

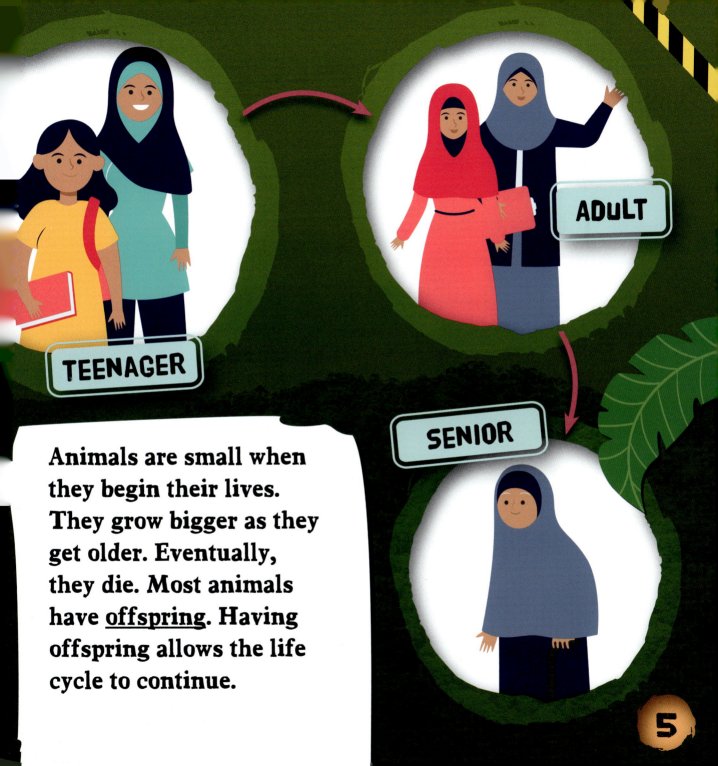

TEENAGER

ADULT

SENIOR

Animals are small when they begin their lives. They grow bigger as they get older. Eventually, they die. Most animals have <u>offspring</u>. Having offspring allows the life cycle to continue.

CHIMPANZEES

Chimpanzees are a type of ape. They live in places with lots of trees. These places include rainforests, woodlands, and grasslands.

CHIMPANZEES ARE ENDANGERED.

Chimpanzees live in large groups called troops. They are very <u>social</u> and smart. They sometimes use sticks as tools to dig and find food. They also use leaves like a cup to drink water.

ENDANGERED ANIMALS

Endangered <u>species</u> are at risk of going extinct. When an animal is extinct, there are none of them left in the world. Many things can cause animals to become endangered.

A habitat is an area where an animal typically lives. Sometimes animals are threatened because they lose their habitat. Animals can also become endangered if humans hunt them too much. Illegal hunting is called poaching.

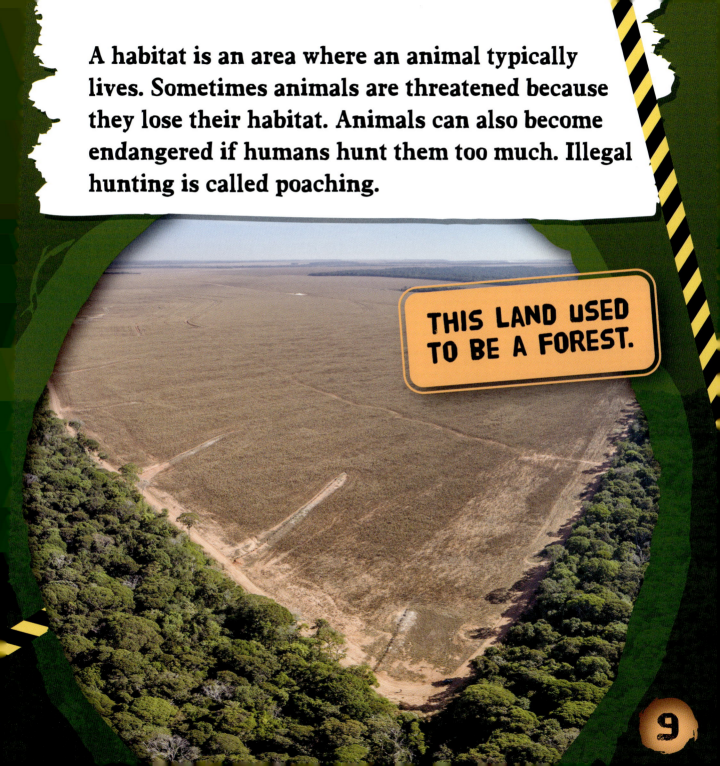

THIS LAND USED TO BE A FOREST.

THE LIFE CYCLE BEGINS

To help chimpanzees, we need to know about their life cycle. Adult chimpanzees need <u>mates</u> for the life cycle to continue. Mates can have young together.

Many chimpanzees have multiple mates each year. A mate is usually someone from their own troop.

BEING BORN

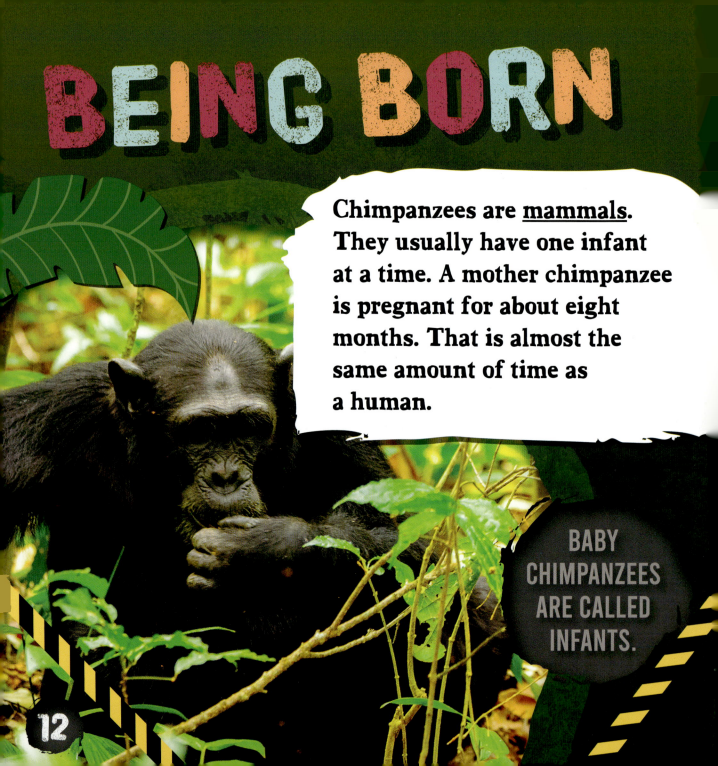

Chimpanzees are <u>mammals</u>. They usually have one infant at a time. A mother chimpanzee is pregnant for about eight months. That is almost the same amount of time as a human.

BABY CHIMPANZEES ARE CALLED INFANTS.

Female chimpanzees give birth alone. They find a quiet place away from the rest of the troop.

INFANTS START DRINKING THEIR MOTHER'S MILK WITHIN HOURS OF BEING BORN.

NEWBORNS

Newborn chimpanzees are not very strong. They need their mothers to look after them. A mother carries her baby everywhere for the first few months of its life.

MOTHERS OFTEN CARRY THEIR INFANTS ON THEIR BACKS.

CHIMPANZEES HAVE STRONG BONDS WITH THEIR MOTHERS.

Chimpanzees learn to walk when they are about six months old. They continue to drink their mother's milk for about four years.

GROWING UP

Chimpanzees learn to live on their own when they are four to five years old. They learn how to build their own nests. They start sleeping alone.

Many chimpanzees continue to have very strong bonds with their mothers. Some still ride on their mothers' backs from time to time.

ADULT LIFE

Adult chimpanzees stay in the troop they were born in. Females can start having infants when they are 13 to 14 years old. Males become adults when they are about 15 years old.

Chimpanzees often have an infant every three to five years. In the wild, they usually live for about 45 years.

DANGERS

Chimpanzees face many dangers. They are killed for their meat. This is one of the main reasons they are endangered.

Chimpanzees are also losing their homes to deforestation. Deforestation is when forests are removed so humans can build things or grow food.

THE LIFE CYCLE CONTINUES

Some people work to make sure that chimpanzees' life cycles can continue. They remove traps that have been set by poachers. Others replant forests to give chimpanzees a new home.

A CONSERVATIONIST IS SOMEONE WHO PROTECTS ANIMALS AND THE ENVIRONMENT.

There are lots of small things you can do to help chimpanzees.
- Don't waste paper. Then, fewer trees will be cut down. This can help stop deforestation.
- Reuse things such as bottles and jars instead of throwing them away. That way, chimpanzees' habitats will not be polluted.

TRY MAKING POTTED PLANTS USING OLD PLASTIC BOTTLES.

GLOSSARY

BONDS — relationships based on love, friendship, and loyalty

ENVIRONMENT — the natural world

MAMMALS — animals that are warm-blooded, have a backbone, and produce milk

MATES — partners of the same species that animals produce young with

OFFSPRING — the young of an animal, a person, or a plant

SOCIAL — to need and enjoy the company of others

SPECIES — a group of very similar animals or plants that can create young together

INDEX

deforestation 21, 23
forests 6, 9, 21–22
habitats 9
infants 12–14, 18–19
life cycles 4–5, 10, 22
mates 10–11
mothers 12–15, 17
troops 7, 11, 13, 18